Marking Time
A Chronicle of Cancer

Valerie Volk

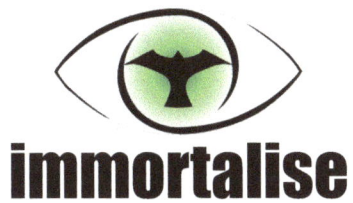

First published in 2020 by Immortalise
contact: info@immortalise.com.au
© Valerie Volk 2020

The moral rights of the author have been asserted.
All rights reserved. Except as permitted under the Australian Copyright Act 1968 (for example, a fair dealing for the purposes of study, research, criticism or review), no part of this book may be reproduced, stored in a retrieval system, communicated or transmitted in any form or by any means without prior written permission. All inquiries should be made to the author.

Author/s:	Valerie Volk
Title:	Marking Time; a Chronicle of Cancer
ISBN:	978-0-6488957-0-1

Subjects: 1 Poetry, 2 Interpersonal Relations, 3 Cancer, 4 Chemotherapy

Cover design by: Ben Morton
Typeset by: Ben Morton
Original photographs by: Simon Bartlett and Valerie Volk
Other photographs sourced from Dreamstime.com and 123RF

For David

with love

Acknowledgements

I acknowledge with gratitude the support of many people in the publication of this book. The alphabetical listing is because all have made varied but significant contributions.

    Simon Bartlett
    Aidan Coleman
    David Harris
    Rosanne Hawke
    Ben Morton
    Russell Schrale
    Lincoln Size
    Felicity Volk
    Mark Worthing

The friends who have travelled the cancer road with us, who encouraged me to make these poems available to a broader audience, including Margaret and Colin Ames, Greta Bird, Jane Greenwood, Jennifer Hand, Anne Jantzen, Janice Staehr, Nicholas Volk, Keith and Jenni Welzel, Anthony Wight, Margaret Young.

    Members of my writing groups who have given invaluable comment on many of the poems in this collection: Friendly Street Poets, Hills Poetry, Literati, Passion of Poets, TramsEnd Poets.

INTRODUCTION

Valerie Volk's poetry never disappoints and *Marking Time - A Chronicle of Cancer* is no exception. This is a beautiful and transparently honest, brave and moving narrative of a journey through lymphoma, a beautiful word, as Volk observes, though deadly.

First, there is the incredulous prognosis, then the limbo, the waiting, the fear, the confinement, inability to eat, losing hair, weight and energy. Above all, the learning of patience, and the thankfulness for love, the quiet gift amongst it all.

Perceptive images personify chemo and cancer cells: coiled snakes, a battleground, military tactics, pulling weeds out by the roots; how the canker in *Hamlet* now has a more sinister meaning, but Hercules fighting the many-head Hydra and winning gives cause for hope.

There is suffering but Volk also provides humour: jokes in the chemo ward and riding the chemo-go-round. It goes round and round, up and down and never stops. Yet there is joy in the simple, ordinary things. A nest of birds offers new meaning; just holding one another in the night is enough; the desire to dance at the word, 'remission'.

The most poignant moment for me is ringing the 'ship's bell' at the end of chemo, a sign of remission, of victory – a peal of hope for all.

I wish I could have read this when we were travelling the same road and I know *Marking Time - A Chronicle of Cancer* will be an inspiration for those still on the journey and for those who want to understand and care.

Rosanne Hawke

Contents

JUNE
    Beforehand   5

JULY
    In the Cancer Clinic   7
    Away from you   9
    Last night   11
    Sharing   13
    Biopsy   15

AUGUST
    Limbo   17
    After the oncologist   19
    With the haematologist   21
    In the Chemo Lab.   23
    An irony   25
    Talking hair   27
    A different ABC   29
    Battle lines   31
    Quo vadis?   33
    At 3 am   35
    Little demons   37
    Military tactics   39
    Cancer gardening   41

SEPTEMBER
    Chemo aftermath.   43
    Marking time   45
    An English Literature lesson   47
    On the ward   49
    Chemo-go-round   51

OCTOBER
- Lessons from the ancient days — 53
- Punctuation — 55
- Cyclical — 57
- Identification — 59
- Barbed wire — 61
- Patient Patience — 63
- In praise of chemo — 65

NOVEMBER
- Cytotoxic — 67
- The gift — 69
- Homecoming — 71
- The return — 73
- Treatment five — 75
- Chemo Sonnet — 77
- Ode to a PICC line — 79

DECEMBER
- December — 81
- Christmas — 83
- Waiting game — 85
- The chill — 87

JANUARY
- Verdict — 89
- Ringing the bell — 91
- Gamesmanship — 93
- Evening at home — 95

Photography Acknowledgements
Also by Valerie Volk

JUNE

Beforehand

Clear blue sky.
Just one small cloud
way off,
on the horizon.

Stray aches and pain …
What can we expect?
A penalty of age.

How did it move to centre sky,
that tiny wisp,
looming high above,
as doctors probe, investigate?
A muscle ache
no more dismissed as trivial
but subject to grave looks.
Then tests, referrals,
phone calls – yes, it's urgent.

That small distant cloud
began to swell, to grow,
until day turned from blue
to dark with thunderclouds
threatening storms to come.

JULY

In the Cancer Clinic

A calm face, non-committal.
Shuffling papers, GP notes,
the first stage test results.
She's keen to double-check,
makes calls to radiologists,
orders another battery
of tests and scans. Remains
a kindly distant presence.
Refuses to be drawn.
Until I see results of these
I really can't say anything
more definite.

We sit confused;
shell-shocked.
Not the life that we had planned.
Where did this come from?
Tsunami sweeping in.
Please pass us by
and leave us on the beach
unscathed.

Away from you

Now I begrudge our hours apart.
Once willingly anticipated,
times of separation –
freedom, independence,
chance to structure my own days
to suit my passing whims,
even pleasures of a solitary bed –
now loom as dark foreshadowing:
some future day may bring,
unwelcomed,
longer hours of solitude.

The pleasures of my freedom
existed only in the certainty
that it was circumscribed, defined,
by knowing that in due course
we would be together.

I, once so independent,
once autonomous,
now like an anxious child
simply crave your nearness,
the reassuring warmth
of being in your arms.

Last night

I dreamed
we sat together at a concert.
Singer's voice,
beauty disembodied,
soaring to the ceiling,
lost in gilded curlicues.
I revelled in our closeness,
responses deepened
in our sharing.

It seemed I left you briefly,
went to greet a friend,
but on returning found
only your empty seat.
An overwhelming sense of loss,
knife thrust of your absence,
an anguished desolation.
When I awoke,
tears had soaked my pillow.

Sharing

Your pain is mine.
When, in the night,
I feel you turn and twist
in bleak distress, or when
sharp stabs pierce
long unending aching hours,
I feel the helplessness
of those who can do nothing but,
as you request, *Be here for me.*

I feel you leave our bed,
and know it has become unbearable,
that somewhere in the house
you, stoic, wait its passing.
I join you, impotent to help,
but just to be with you.

Those moments when at last
drugs take effect, and briefly
there's relief,
those moments are a benediction
for us both.

Biopsy

Biopsy …
a curious word.
It rolls upon the tongue
with deceptive ease.
But this, says our oncologist,
will give some answers.

They take a sample,
(of course I've gone to Google…)
some tissue for analysis,
for other tests may indicate,
but this will make
a certain diagnosis possible.
Delicate insertion of a needle
and somewhere now
an expert seeks an answer.

Once again we wait.
Another three days pass.
Uncertainty
harder to endure
than knowledge?

AUGUST

Limbo

Not the sixties dance,
nor the Play Dead game,
though it too is a puzzle platform.
Our limbo's different,
another waiting time,
known to all trapped souls.
On Friday afternoon
she had been measured, cautious.
There'll be more tests.

Come back on Monday.
Then we'll know much more.

Three days of limbo.
But at last it's Monday.
I drive home from the gym.
Still dark, the pre-dawn hush.
Traffic lights ahead.
If they stay green
until I get there,
everything will turn out well.

I rev the engine
try to make it,
but it's orange…
red too quickly.
Now I sit here at the lights,
waiting for the change,
another limbo,
cursing yet again
my superstitious soul.

After the oncologist

Lymphoma –
such a lovely word.
Melodious. Seductive.
But so deadly.
Quietly it infiltrates,
fastening upon
your unsuspecting bones
until pain brings awareness
of its presence.
Coiled like a snake
for twenty years
waiting, waiting …
Now it strikes,
to catch us unawares.
And suddenly lives change.
We see the future,
if not darkly,
through a foggy glass.

With the haematologist

He's cautious, clinical,
explains precisely,
choosing words with care,
exactly what is happening.

A haematologist, we know.
A man of science, quite detached.
He says you were an engineer
so tailors carefully
his explanations
in terms that are mathematical.
Systems analysis – your field –
your body as a complex system.
You like this, I can see.

But inside I rebel in fury:
He's not just flesh and blood,
this man I love,
whose body I have known,
have touched,
explored with tender fingers,
brought to ecstasy.

Show me that beyond the scans
that loom so ominously,
dark patches on the screen,
beyond your forecast figures,
prognosis given with reluctance,
you see him as a person,
a living breathing loving
Man

In the Chemo Lab.

First steps into a new life.
Cancer's domain.
Friendly sympathetic nurses.
Careful leading to the chairs,
set in serried ranks.
Occupants look up,
leave their private worlds;
smile at our tentative glances.
Are we so clearly new to this?
New routines as drips are hooked
to long tubes with your arm.
Hours pass. We talk, read,
do the crosswords saved for this.
The day drags on …

An irony

The Chinese nurse,
focused and smiling,
adjusts the needles, lines and drip.
Carefully she places a new bag
within the frame above your head.
Important now, she orders,
you keep your arm quite still.
We don't want any drop of this one
to escape outside your vein.
It's beautiful, she says,
eyeing with approval
the bag, a soft attractive mauve.
It's beautiful, but deadly.

It hangs there, poised aloft,
death bearing.
This is an irony:
they poison you to save you.

Talking hair

I think I'd like a beret ...
So Gallic, I agree.
You'll look quite chic.
But our oncologist seems disapproving.
Perhaps he thinks such levity
misplaced. A serious discussion:
side-effects of chemo.
Can he not understand this?
To cope with bad news,
dire forebodings,
laughter is our weapon.

We ask with interest:
All hair goes with chemo?
Head, body, legs?
Now he is reassuring.
Head hair first. Others slowly.
It all grows back. Head first,
sometimes curly.
Bit by bit the rest.

Not *'easy come and easy go'*,
we quip. *The other way.*
Easy go, and easy come?
At last he offers an uneasy smile.

A different ABC

This language is intriguing.
Words that I had known
as neutral, even friendly,
words like *multitude* and *myriad*
suggest a generosity, a richness –
but not when they refer
to cancer cells.

Others now assume a different quality.
Words like *aggressive* –
always minatory, yes, yet now
so hostile, threatening.
But *avid* …? Once it had a sense
of 'eager', almost a positive.
No more. For now I understand
an avid cancer – one that hungers
for your bones, that eats away
their surface, leaving just
long stretches of erosion.
Black patches on the scan.
Lace-like. These are not
a thing of beauty.

Battle lines

Your body is a battleground.
Cancer cells advantaged –
they had first choice
and took the best positions.
Waited stealthily,
sent spies and outriders,
infiltrating tissues, bones.

Now we amass our armies;
an array of drugs that drip
from chemo tubes,
gather strength,
prepare for battle.

These are not Arnold's armies,
ignorant, who clash by night.
No, these are cognisant:
theirs aware of weaknesses;
ours using all manoeuvres known
to medicine and science
in this battle.

Quo vadis?

The days are empty.
We are adrift
on an uncertain sea.
Each day together
still a gift we share.
But now horizons waver
mists obscure our vision
we cling together
like children frightened
of the dark.

At 3 am

Lying awake beside you,
both of us silent,
eyes obdurately open,
staring into a future
not yet revealed.
Our cup of tea at 3 am,
by now a ritual,
laughter provoking
among our friends,
remains a comfort.
Tea has been found
in ancient monuments.
Some things are permanent.

Little demons

Cancer cells are cunning.
Predatory, active,
and malevolent.
They spread insistently,
multiplying.
They take control.

Reports use words
we've come to hate.
Avid and *aggressive* –
we see them as an enemy.

How are you? people ask.
You answer stoically.
But quietly, alone with me,
you use the word '*incredulous.*'
We are.
How did this happen?
Is it real?

Military tactics

A standard ploy for armies
under strong attack.
Now reinforcements come.
No more just cancer cells.
I see instead the supplementary forces.
Proliferation of red spots;
your body's surface pock-marked,
a shrapnel siege from outside.
And inner battles rage,
as teeth ache fiercely,
stomach churns. As warned,
all appetites now wane.
Each day is wearisome.
The enemy creates a slow attrition,
saps life of pleasure by fatigue
that makes each act a challenge.
This is a many-fronted war,
and all combines to undermine
the strength of your defences.
Now covertly the central forces
strive to take new ground:
cancer cells attempt proliferation,
opposing all your efforts to counter
with chemotherapy's defences.

Cancer gardening

I crouch down in the drive.
Weeds flourish in the cracks
between the sun-baked bricks.
Tenacious little devils
but I scrape and tug.
Kindly neighbours wave
from passing cars, and smile.
Friends stop, call out advice.
You could spray those, you know.
But shake their heads –
I'm known as OCD.

Each weed that comes,
complete with roots intact,
I breathe a sigh of triumph,
grimly satisfied.
But when roots break
and just torn scraps emerge
I shiver slightly.
I think of you in cancer ward.
Complete eradication of that weed
will mean a chemo victory,
another cancer cell destroyed.
No traces left. Your time in chairs
hooked up to deadly drips
complete success. But if the root
remains inviolate …

Another neighbour passes,
smiles to see my foolish task.
Do they not understand
this is my crystal ball,
and these my tarot cards?

SEPTEMBER

Chemo aftermath.

Bad chemo day.
Your face is grey and drawn,
profile hawk-like,
lines etched more deeply,
eyes sunken
under what were once your brows.

We sit outside,
sun's warmth a comfort
in this time of pain.
Easy for me to say:
This too will pass.
A bad few days,
we know the pattern.
You grimace
at my feeble effort.

But then above
high in the huge old palm
we hear a magpie carol,
watch the two birds come,
working together,
build their nest.

The sun is warm
birds sing
for all around is life,
with scurrying ants
and scent of freesias in the air.

More eloquent
than any words of mine.

Marking time

Bird flutters to the gabled roof
across the road. Sits at its peak.
Waits.
Poised.
For what?

I sit beside your chemo chair,
watch you sleep,
fettered to the drip,
with thin red line of poison
running to your arm.
One toxin to attack another.
Doxorubicin.
It's an army of red devils
fiercely marching
to send those cancer cells
in panicked flight.

We wait.
We're marking time.
In schoolyards of my childhood
so we waited. Scrubbed faces,
pig-tailed little girls,
scab-kneed scruffy boys,
straggly lines of six-year-olds,
queued for entry to the classrooms.
Mark time, children!
Little legs, rising, falling,
marching on the spot.
Marking time.

Today we're marching on the spot,
waiting to see if chemo does its work.

We're marking time, again.

An English Literature lesson

Nights are long, in treatment weeks.
Time hangs heavy, as we wait grey dawns.
We seek distraction in our pasts.
Tell me, you say, *about your school.*
What were you like at school?

I tell you of my English class,
of *Hamlet* on hot summer afternoons.
I see myself, a studious girl,
the sort who always had a question,
raise my hand to ask.

Our English teacher looked confused,
a temporary hesitation …
There may well be a link.
But Shakespeare's word is 'canker' –
same idea. Something destructive.
We scrutinised the line.
An earnest class, grappling with old words.

'The canker galls the infants of the spring.'
Now girls, he means the buds.
Ophelia's brother warns her
that dangers could destroy her innocence.

Strange how these things come back.
Here, lying in the dark, old words still haunt.
Today we have our modern 'canker'.
It too wreaks havoc and destruction,
as cancer cells eat into bones,
your innocent bones.

On the ward

Reception nurse looks up and greets us.
Chair Fifteen today, smiling brightly.
In here they smile a lot.
Warmly, kindly, reassuringly.

Fifteen's a half way number.
This ward is big,
warehouse size,
a cancer factory.
Its stations numbered,
one to twenty eight.
Cancer is an industry,
its workers, chained to benches,
have their set routines
with catheters inserted,
pills distributed,
pulses taken, temperatures,
the endless litany of questions:
Name? Date of birth? Address?
checked and double-checked all day …

We walk to Chair Fifteen.
Drips are linked, bags of lethal fluids
hooked aloft, a blanket brought,
and so we settle for
another working day.

Chemo-go-round

A ride you didn't choose,
but now discover you're astride
a prancing pony as it bucks and sways.
Around us fairground music blares

oblivious in their merry-making.
I watch you from the sidelines
as, with stoic calm, you bear
the unanticipated ups and downs
of cancer-dominated life.
These cycles come, begin,
run their appointed course.
A chemo bout, then follow
good days, just a few,
until the poison does its work
and total abject misery
swamps every part of life.
A gradual resurfacing,
until the cycle starts once more.

This funfair ride is not a treat,
although the ticket's cost is high.
It sure belies its name –
there's not much merriment,
although it may go round and round …

OCTOBER

Lessons from the ancient days

Now even shortest walks are hard.
But yet you crave
the sight of sea, and rippling water,
horizon lines that blur,
the more we concentrate our eyes.

Slow-footed at sand's edge,
watching ceaseless to and fro
of never-ending waves,
we reach the rockpools
where a single crab scuttles
seeking shelter of the ledge.

Cancer, we ruminate, the crab.
That sign we've come to fear.
So powerful, the ancients thought.
A scarab beetle, or a tortoise,
it pushed the sun across the sky,
solstice bringing. So powerful.

It is.

But Hercules was not distracted
when Hera's giant crab clung to his foot.
Instead, he fought the many-headed Hydra
and he won!
So even in mythology the crab
could fail its mission of destruction.

A thought that gives us hope.

Punctuation

Life now in three week units.
Third Fridays always treatment days,
tethered to machines all day.
These are the semi-colons.
The weeks between these markers
an ellipsis …
Three dots.
Each is a waiting time,
paused by the comma weekly blood test.
In these periods we hover
in a limbo land.

Ellipses.
Something is indeed left out:
senses impaired,
feelings and sensation jeopardised.
'Bleaching' you have called it.
My world is chemo-bleached.
Taste gone; no sense of smell;
sight and hearing less clear.
Nothing in my world precise;
All is faded.
As for libido – don't go there.

So these weeks are indeed elliptical.
Things that make life full and rich
have gone. So much is now left out.
We wait in eagerness for endings.
No more chemo. Restoration.
Time then for the full stop!

Cyclical

So indeed it is.
Life, I mean.
One cycle ends,
another starts.

Your Round 4 chemo over,
so today we sit outside
luxuriating in the still hot sun
that floods the front veranda.
Three weeks before Round 5.

But while we sit and ruminate,
high above us in the hollow
between palm branches
magpies swoop and dive
feeding their three chicks
whose hungry beaks poke
greedily above nest's edge.

Another cycle,
one that reassures.
My camera always ready.
I place this photo
next to yesterday's
of you hooked up to drips
inside the cancer ward.

Identification

What do they do all day?

We speculate,
our gazes fixed upon the nest
where three chicks wait,
squawking, greedy.
What do they think about?
Too young to move beyond the nest,
high in the towering palm.
No room to play, no toys,
not even a Gameboy.
Just feeling hunger pangs
until, a black/white feathered flurry,
beak laden, mother swoops again.
A non-stop job, she's busy
all day long.

Confined to quarters, I observe.
Yes. You survey the nest,
from your recovery chair in sunshine
on our front veranda.
I know just how that feels.
But it's the nestlings you're observing.
I watch the mother, her incessant task.
Yes, I know how that feels …

Barbed wire

I watch you disappear.
Each day my careful question
as you step on bathroom scales,
Today?
but every day your weight
is further down. Five kilos
worried me. At ten I panicked;
now I see you, gaunt,
thin-faced and hollow-cheeked,
eleven kilos gone in these few weeks.

It's like a ball of wire,
of barbed wire, in my stomach.
Your way with words makes it
so clear it's agonising.
You tell me you are hungry.
One mouthful, two – and then,
the old familiar cry of near despair.
I'm sorry, love. It won't go down.
Not just your sense of taste, but worse:
impossible to swallow.

Your doctor is concerned.
Tomorrow, an endoscopy.
Meanwhile, I watch you disappear,
become a wraith, where every action
is exhausting, where vigour
is a distant memory, and food
a challenge that defeats. I grieve,
for there is nothing I can do.
My natural role, to feed the ones I love,
superfluous, irrelevant, a loss
that saddens as I watch you disappear.
Each night I wonder:
What will you weigh tomorrow?

Patient Patience

Sometimes a word can
startle with exactness –
patient –
and so we are.

Outside the doctor's rooms
sitting in Reception areas
while hours pass.
Wait for doctors, nurses,
specialists of many breeds,
blood tests and scan results.
Oh yes, we're patients.

So we learn the needed lesson:
patience.
So apt.
Another skill acquired
in this long long journey.
We're patient patients.
A needed learning curve.

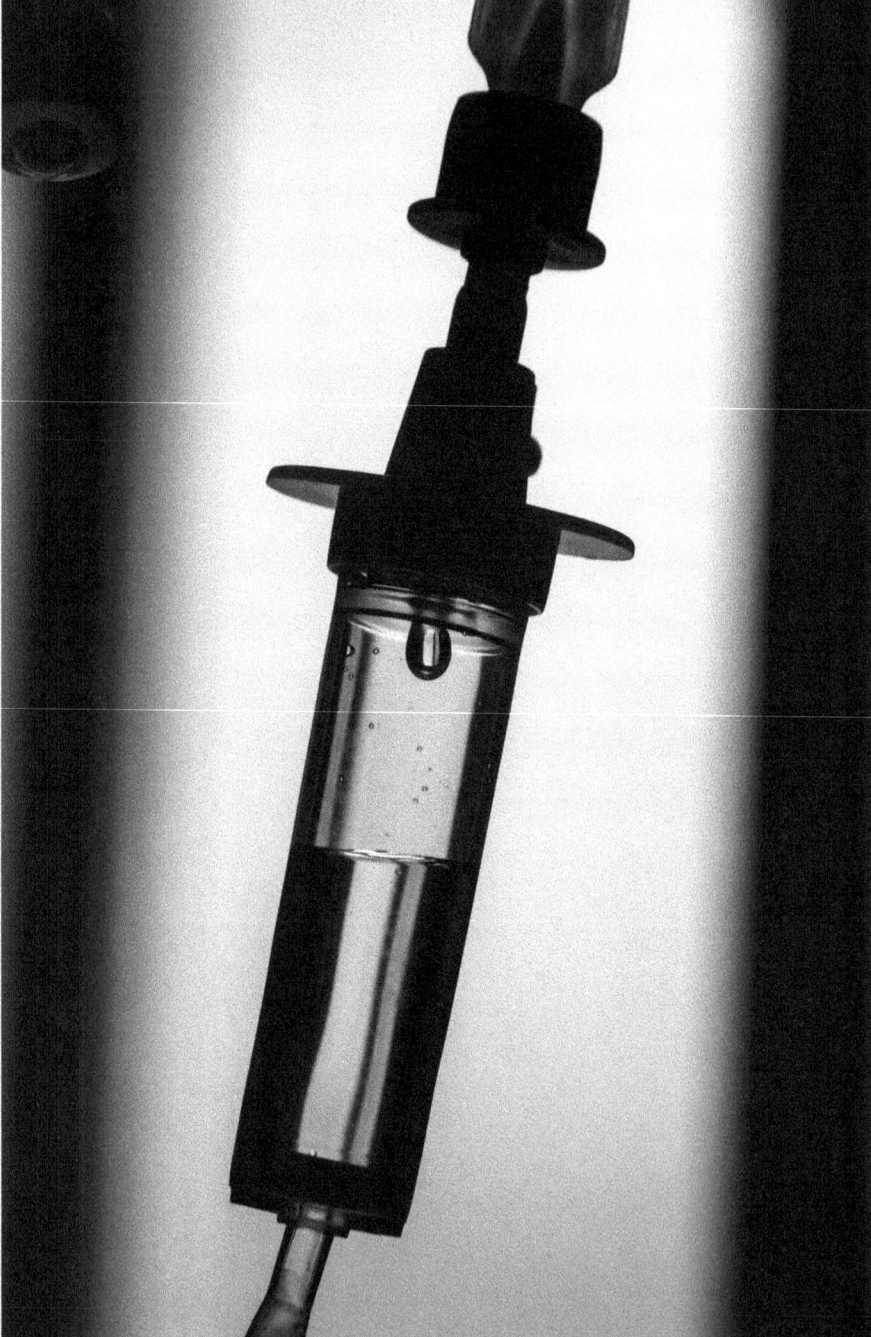

In praise of chemo

CHOP-R
Once a dreaded acronym –
it signifies this lethal substance
dripped into your veins.
But now
CHOP-R's no longer feared.
Scan results have shown us
that it's working.
Those ominous black areas
displayed in old PET scans
way back, two months ago,
have shrunk, are shrinking,
as poison does its work.
CHOP-R now sounds to us
almost benign.

NOVEMBER
Cytotoxic

So suddenly!
Caught unawares.
dramatic moment:
ominous music, darkening picture,
while looking in the other corner
from behind
a killer springs.

How did this happen?
Your doctor's face is grave.
He murmurs:
Unexpected – this reaction.

Then, rapidly, you're 'critical',
rushed into CCU –
the old 'Intensive Care'.
Festooned in PICC lines, drips,
hooked to machines that whirr and buzz,
bags of blood and saline
with their incessant drip,
while nurses, gloved and masked,
keep constant watch.

You're cytotoxic.
It says so on your door.
A warning sign to all who enter here.
I learn a new word:
Methotrexate joins our lexicon.
It's only later that they tell us
how life-threatening this has been.
Alarmed, I find myself each night
offering bewildered prayers.

The gift

A gift you give me:
to be needed.
To see your face turn to me
with relief,
to see your eyes light
as I enter through your door,
to hear you say
My day starts now,
to know that I am wanted.

A morning like last week –
You called me in the early hours.
I woke at once,
phone stowed beside my bed,
and heard you say:
A wretched night.
I know the time
but can you come?

To walk through sleeping streets
in hushed grey early light
through wide glass doors,
dawn bustle of the hospital,
past orderlies with trolleys,
nurses busy with routines of morning –
charts, pulses, temperatures.
I reach Intensive Care,
your special nurse nods to me,
It wasn't a good night.
He's been distressed.
Your eyes are watching for me
lighting your face.
You smile through pain.
To know you need me –
it's a gift you give.

Homecoming

They say you can come home today.
I'm waiting for the call,
cooking all your favourite dishes,
hoping to put flesh back on your bones.
You're frailer, yes, more gaunt,
but smiling still.

A bad two weeks – so unforeseen,
this prolonged hospital stay.
Final revelation as you left,
just how precarious the time.
Now that foreboding figure
with his scythe
is banished, and we smile again.

I'm planning dinner,
baking slices, biscuits - and even,
(just because I love you!)
I've gone to buy your favourites –
time-honoured stalwarts,
Arnott's famed Milk Arrowroots!

The return

I touch your body in the night.
Strange territory now
all bones and angles
where once was soft warm flesh.
It's unfamiliar –
like this cancer realm
that we, uncertainly,
explore each day with cautious steps
between the dark trees, looming.
You're frailer, gaunter.
I watch the scales uneasily:
every morning further down.
But then at night you turn to me,
your arm around my body,
your hands that cup my breast,
suddenly not strange,
no more an unmapped land.

Treatment five

Once more a challenge to endurance –
first night after treatment often is.
Yesterday fifth cycle.
They've pumped you full of poison,
four hours of dripping menace,
dealing death to cancer cells.
Internal war is raging.
You turn, twist, mutter.
No comfort anywhere,
you're in and out of bed.
Frequent thirst,
bedside water bottle filled,
emptied, filled again.
Stomach roiling, its own protest,
vehement resistance to this battle.
No wonder night is torment.

Yet still you turn to me to say
So sorry to disturb your sleep.
Oh my dear one, the real distress
is that there's nothing I can do
except be here for you.

Chemo Sonnet

Shall I compare this to a battleground?
Your warfare now is of a different kind.
Not weapons nor the bugle's clarion sound,
But subtly made assaults on flesh and mind.

Each chemo cycle brings a new attack.
Your chair is tethered to a death machine.
Once started there's no chance of going back,
Unstoppable and toxic, this routine.

Insidious the impact on your brain.
The battle there has power to dismay.
Thoughts scrambled, sense and logic sought in vain,
Sharp intellect blurs further with each day.

So long as chemo works, and cells renew,
This suffering gives future life to you.

Ode to a PICC line

When they first talked about
insertion of a PICC line,
I really didn't understand at all.
They patiently explained it:
Peripherally Inserted Central Catheter.
Doesn't scan, I know,
and didn't make much sense.

But I've learned now to live with this:
as weeks go by
I've come to value how these little tubes
that dangle from your forearm
save frequent needle punctures,
making your life easier.
A nuisance, yes, when showering.
Can catch on sleeves when dressing.
Trivial, such minor irritations
when compared
to constant needles thrusts.

Oh PICC line, you are now a part
of this man whom I love.
I'd even chance the comment that
I love you too …

DECEMBER

December

Festive season everywhere.
Eager shoppers, office parties,
an atmosphere of celebration
as Christmas Day approaches.
A time of expectation.

For us, routines go on.
Another chemo treatment.
Christmas dinner an ordeal
while all around are joyous.

Treatment cycles coming to an end.
Final tests to come.
Foreboding.
What will they bring?
For us too, time of expectation.
We wait, not for a star or shepherds,
but for a different sort of news.

Christmas

Angels round the Christmas tree.
Fragile glass
deftly woven cane
or delicate in tracery of wire.
Collection spanning many years
guards our tree each Christmas.

No thought last year
of changes this one brings.
For now we add new angels
from a different source.
They do not circle 'round the tree
but are our other guardians.
White-garbed, the nurses of the clinic
are also angels.

Waiting game

We wait.
And wonder.
Covert glances at each other
when we count the days.
Next PET scan Tuesday.
On Friday the result.
Was six months' chemo
worth the misery?
From this battleground
how have you emerged?

Meanwhile we talk about a future
bright with promise.
Travel plans that may still happen.
(We haven't cancelled bookings.)
Optimistic messages
to enquiring friends.
And to each other.

But in these count-down days
as Friday looms,
we wait.
And secretly,
we wonder.

The chill

They try to make them friendly –
waiting rooms in hospitals.
Pictures on the walls,
soft décor, comfy chairs,
and even TV thoughtfully
turned low, with teletext.
Why then so cold?
Why arctic temperatures,
a chill that seeps into your bones,
after they have taken him away?

I wait. I contemplate.
Is he too cold? Or do
warm blankets they provide,
keep at bay this chill?
It's 'nuclear', this medicine;
Hours pass; I think about the scans,
X-rays, the imaging, and wonder also:
what are they finding?

More than just temperature
now chills the heart.

JANUARY

Verdict

It's almost like a dance
along the corridor.
We hug close to ourselves
words the doctor spoke.
Complete remission.
Contemplation of that screen;
never has computer monitor
brought such happiness.
Your torso, bones, all clear,
death-carrying black patches
nowhere to be seen.
Best possible result,
his voice comes from a distance
and, for once, he smiles.

We dance light-footed
down the corridor,
But it is lined with chairs
and faces grey with care.
It would be too indecent
to show our bubbling joy,
so, sobered now,
we slow our steps.

Ringing the bell

Six months chemo – final day.
They're taking out your PICC line.
We look around the clinic
almost with a fondness –
a place we know so well.
Today all chairs are occupied,
all twenty-eight.
Masked nurses bustle 'round
pushing trolleys full of deadly stuff.
Patients doze, read papers,
chat idly to supportive friends.
Some sport bright scarves and caps,
beanies ever popular,
others flaunt bald heads –
but all look worn.

Today you leave,
so at this last farewell
you get to ring the bell,
that brass bell on the wall
adjoining the Reception Desk
where grey-faced newcomers report.
Tradition, this.
Departing patients, cured –
or in remission –
get to ring the old ship's bell,
a sign of victory.
We want it to resound today
throughout this chemo world,
a peal of hope for all.
It is, for us.

Gamesmanship

Thoughtful now,
we pause to pay attention
to his words.
A cautious man, our haematologist.
Reflect upon his letter.
Lymphoma is not curable.
We understand his prudence.
Remission. Not a guarantee.

For now, his skill has triumphed.
Gladiator like, he fought the beast.
His edge? Power to predict, to plan.
But lions will fight back.
One day, this monster too
may rear its head once more,
the deadly contest be replayed.

For now, the contest's over.
Outcome, a win.
So we exult in triumph
and live in hope.

Evening at home

Notes cascade, rippling
as your fingers move
across the keys.
I sit, content to listen.
Your stops and starts
and fumbling notes
are dear to me.
For this is what the year has been,
a time of hesitations, fears;
it too, like this your music,
has come to resolution.
I sit at peace,
a glow of quiet happiness.
It is now possible
to look ahead in confidence,
foresee years of serenity
that for a time seemed jeopardised.
Play on, for as the music flows,
my heart is filled with gratitude,
and I give thanks to God.

PHOTOGRAPHY ACKNOWLEDGEMENTS

Source   page number and details

Simon Bartlett: 4, 6, 8, 10, 12, 14, 20, 22, 24, 28, 30, 32, 34, 36, 38, 42, 48, 52, 54, 58, 66, 68, 70, 72, 74, 76, 78, 80, 82, 84, 86, 88. 92, 94

Valerie Volk: 18, 26, 40, 90

Dreamstime.com: cover   ID: 13475709 © Chepko
                16   ID: 176071116 © Jan Zwoliński
                44   ID: 47092514 © Majivecka
                46   ID: 41757975 © Type01
                50   ID: 17501333 © Terhox
                56   ID: 173909658 © Christopher Bellette
                62   ID: 3695829 © Maa-illustrations
                64   ID: 160629013 © Daboost

123RF: 60   ID: 30102184 © James Heyworth

ALSO BY VALERIE VOLK

In Due Season - Poems of love and loss Pantaenus Press, 2009
A Promise of Peaches Ginninderra Press, 2011
Even Grimmer Tales Interactive Press, 2012
Passion Play - the Oberammergau Tales Wakefield Press, 2013
Flowers & Forebears Ginninderra Press, 2014
Indochina Days Ginninderra Press, 2015
Bystanders Wakefield Press, 2015
Of Llamas and Piranhas Ginninderra Press, 2017
In Search of Anna, Wakefield Press, 2019

www.ingramcontent.com/pod-product-compliance
Lightning Source LLC
Chambersburg PA
CBHW040243010526
44107CB00065B/2853